BLAST OFF!
URANUS

Helen and David Orme

Copyright © ticktock Entertainment Ltd 2007
First published in Great Britain in 2006 by ticktock Media Ltd.,
Unit 2, Orchard Business Centre, North Farm Road,
Tunbridge Wells, Kent, TN2 3XF

ticktock project editor: Julia Adams
ticktock project designer: Emma Randall

We would like to thank: Sandra Voss, Tim Bones, James Powell,
Indexing Specialists (UK) Ltd.

ISBN 978 1 84696 054 3
Printed in China
A CIP catalogue record for this book is available from the British Library.

Picture credits
t=top, b=bottom, c=centre, l-left, r=right, bg=background
Hubble Space Telescope: 17tr, 19 all; NASA: 1 all, 7tr, 7c, 7bl, 8, 13 all, 14 all, 15 all, 16, 20, 22 all, 23b; Science Photo Library:
front cover, 4/5bg (original), 12, 21, 23t; Shutterstock: 2/3bg, 7tl, 9b, 18b, 24bg; ticktock picture archive: 5tr, 6/7bg, 6, 9t,
10/11bg, 10, 11 all, 14/15bg, 17b, 18/19bg, 18bl, 22/23bg;
Every effort has been made to trace the copyright holders, and we apologise in advance for any unintentional omissions.
We would be pleased to insert the appropriate acknowledgements in any subsequent edition of this publication.

Contents

Where is Uranus?

There are eight planets in our solar system. The planets travel around the Sun. Uranus is the seventh planet from the Sun.

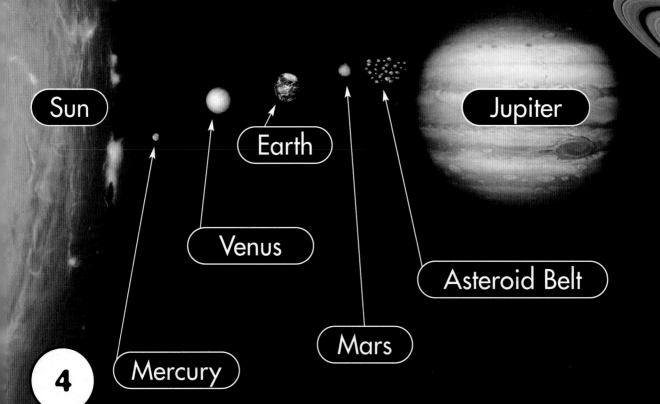

Sun

Earth

Jupiter

Venus

Asteroid Belt

Mars

Mercury

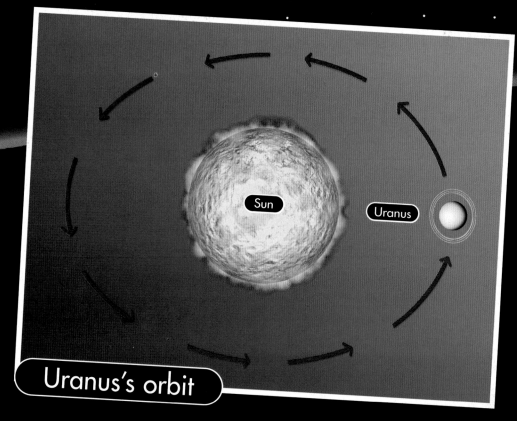

Uranus's orbit

Uranus travels around the Sun once every 84 **Earth years**. This journey is called its **orbit**. The time it takes for a planet to travel around the Sun once is called a **year**.

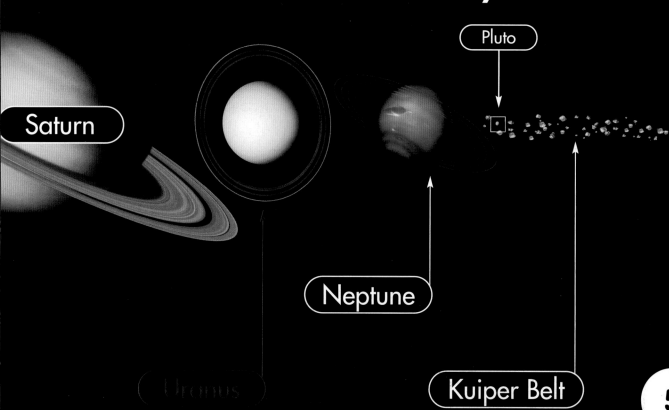

Pluto

Saturn

Neptune

Kuiper Belt

Uranus

Planet Facts

The centre of Uranus is made of rock and possibly ice. The rest of the planet is made up of gases and **liquid** water.

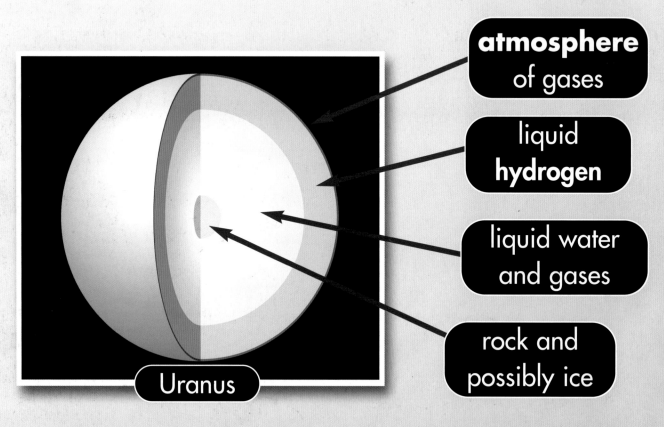

atmosphere of gases

liquid **hydrogen**

liquid water and gases

rock and possibly ice

Uranus

The **methane gas** makes Uranus look blue when we look at the planet through a telescope.

12,756 km

Earth

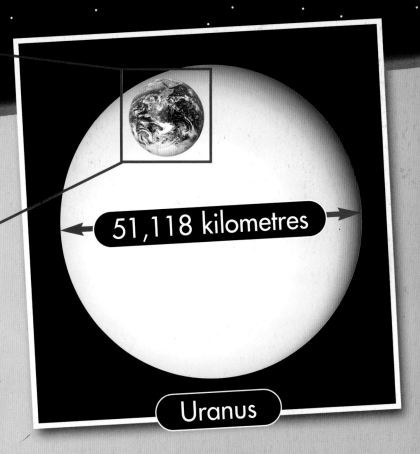
51,118 kilometres

Uranus

Uranus is the third biggest planet in the **solar system**.

Planets are always spinning. Some planets spin like this.

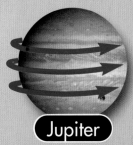
Jupiter

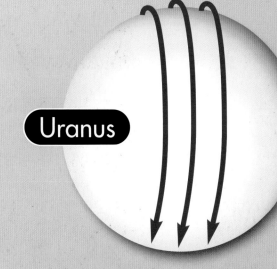
Uranus

Uranus is tilted on its side, so it spins like this! It was probably once hit by another object the size of a planet, which knocked it over.

A day is the time it takes a planet to spin around once. A day on Uranus is the same as 17 ½ hours on Earth.

Uranus is a very windy planet. Cold clouds made of **hydrogen gas** and **methane gas** race around the planet.

clouds

gassy **atmosphere**

The clouds travel at up to 644 kilometres an hour!

A **year** on Uranus lasts 84 **Earth years**. This means that the seasons last about 21 years!

The **atmosphere** of Uranus is cold, but near the centre it is very, very hot.

centre
4,982 °C

atmosphere
-214 °C

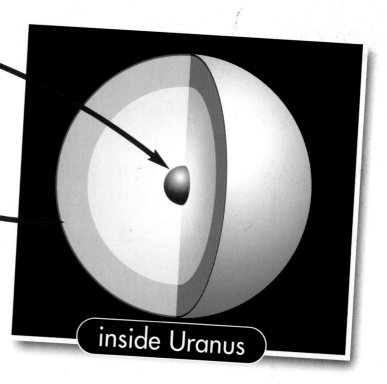

inside Uranus

The lowest temperature ever reached on Earth is -89 °C.

When methane gas is squeezed under pressure, very hard tiny diamonds can be produced. Some scientists think it might rain diamonds on Uranus!

Uranus in History

Some planets have been known about for thousands of years, because people could see them in the sky. Uranus was not discovered until just over 200 years ago.

Uranus was the first planet to be discovered using a telescope. It was discovered by the English **astronomer** William Herschel in 1781.

Herschel designed and built his own telescopes.

Herschel's telescope

King George III

Herschel lived in Britain. He named the planet George's Star after George III, the British king.

The planet was later renamed Uranus, after the ancient Greek god of the sky.

Looking for Moons

Uranus has 27 moons that we know about. Our Earth only has one! The moons are named after characters from the plays of the famous English writer William Shakespeare.

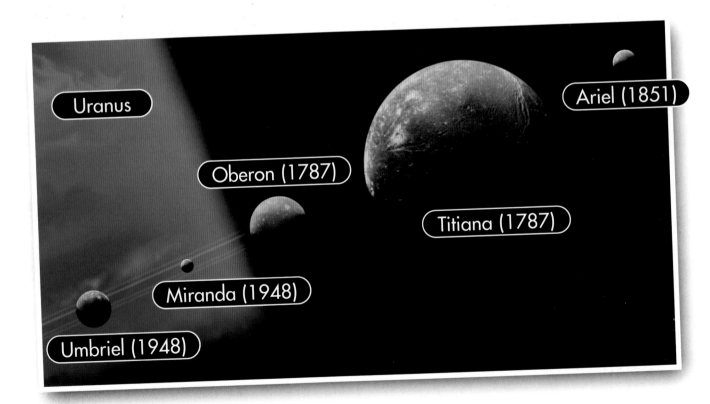

Uranus

Ariel (1851)

Oberon (1787)

Titiana (1787)

Miranda (1948)

Umbriel (1948)

This painting shows Uranus's five biggest moons and when they were discovered. These moons were first seen through telescopes.

In 1986, the **space probe** Voyager 2 discovered another 10 moons.

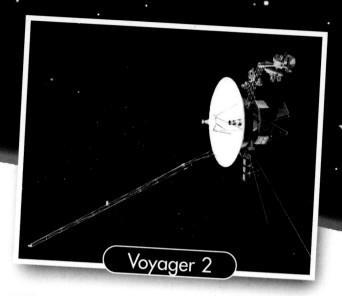

Voyager 2

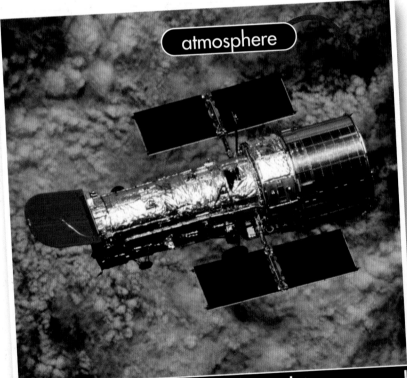

atmosphere

This is Hubble above Earth's atmosphere

The **Hubble Space Telescope** has discovered a further 12 small moons around Uranus! Some were not found until 2003.

Hubble can see Uranus's smallest moons even though they measure just 16 kilometres across and are about 4 ½ billion km from Earth!

Uranus's Biggest Moons

Scientists think Uranus's five biggest moons are made of ice and rock.

The two biggest moons Oberon and Titania were discovered by William Herschel.

576 km

Titania

3476 km

Miranda

483 km

Earth's Moon

1522 km

Oberon

Nine separate photographs of different sections of Miranda were slotted together by a computer to make this photograph.

Miranda

These photographs of Uranus's moons were taken by the Voyager 2 **space probe** in 1986.

Uranus's Rings

Uranus has a system of rings made of dust and rocks. **Astronomers** found the first rings in 1977.

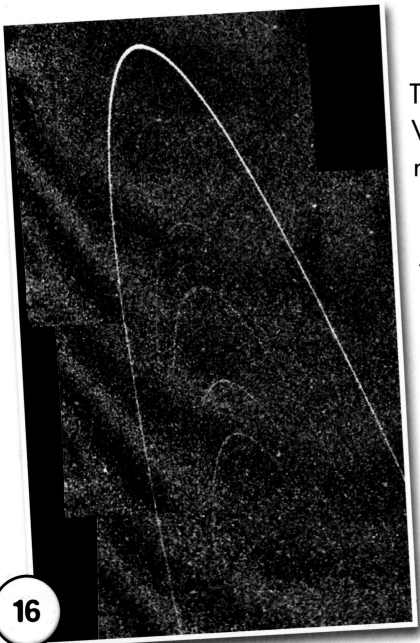

The **space probe** Voyager 2 found more rings in 1986.

This picture of Uranus's rings is made up of many small photographs. They were joined together by a computer. The photos where taken by Voyager 2.

In December 2005, the **Hubble Space Telescope** discovered more rings.

Scientists think that when Uranus's moons are hit by rocks, dust and stones fly off into space and become part of the rings.

Hubble photograph

Rings

Moons

This painting shows how the rings would look close up.

Studying Uranus is difficult because it is so far from Earth. Scientists sometimes use maths to work out what Uranus is like.

If you know exactly where to look, Uranus can be seen in the night sky. It looks like a very distant star.

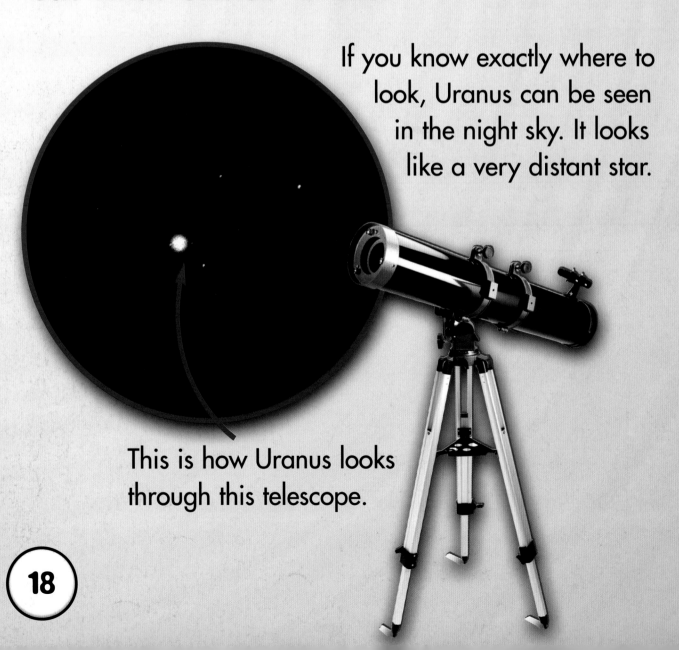

This is how Uranus looks through this telescope.

The best photographs of Uranus come from the **Hubble Space Telescope**.

Hubble photographs

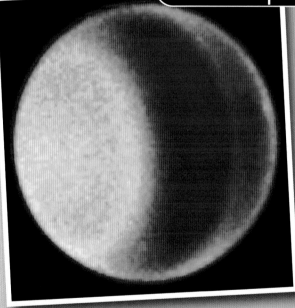

This photograph has been coloured red on a computer. You can see the bands of clouds around the planet.

Because Hubble is outside of Earth's **atmosphere**, its pictures are much clearer than pictures from even the biggest telescopes on Earth.

19

Voyager 2 is the only space mission there has been to Uranus. Voyager 2 discovered some of the planet's moons and that Uranus is tilted.

Titan-Centaur rocket

TITAN/CENTAUR COMPLEX 41

Voyager 2 was blasted into space aboard a Titan-Centaur rocket on 20th August, 1977.

The launch was at Cape Canaveral in Florida, USA.

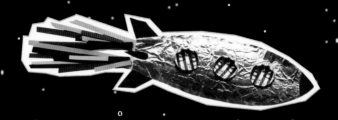

Voyager 2 reached Jupiter in 1979, Saturn in 1981 and Uranus in 1986.

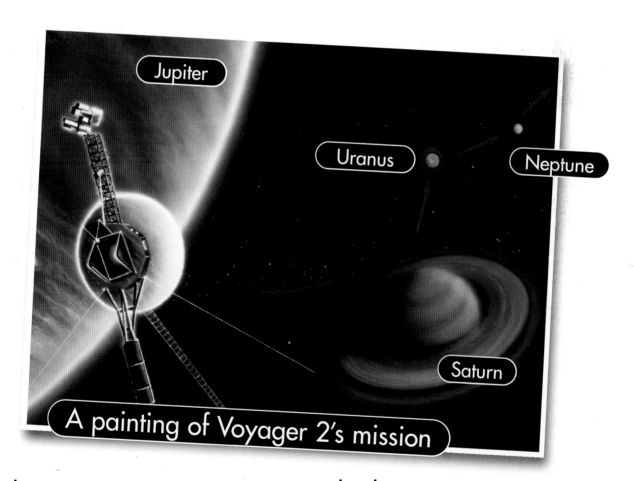

Jupiter

Uranus

Neptune

Saturn

A painting of Voyager 2's mission

Then, in 1989, Voyager 2 reached Neptune. It is now at the edge of our **solar system**. Hopefully it will send information back to Earth until 2030.

Future Missions

Scientists are certain it is too cold for life on Uranus, but they would like to find out more about the planet. At the moment, there are no new missions planned.

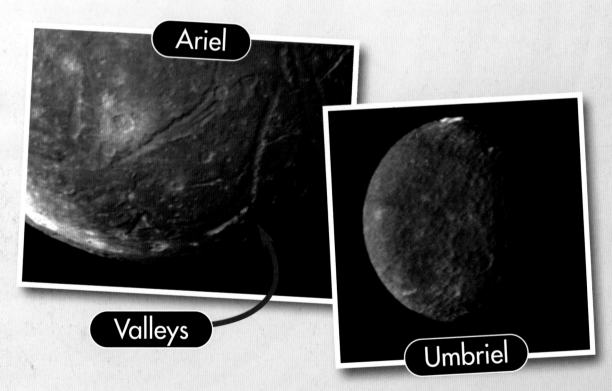

Ariel

Valleys

Umbriel

Scientists would like a closer look at Uranus's moons to find out why their surfaces are so different. There might even be more moons to find!

Any missions to Uranus will be done by robots. If **astronauts** went, it would take nearly nine years to get there, and nine years to come back again!

a painting of Uranus and its rings

Voyager 2 is carrying a special disc. It contains information and greetings from Earth. This is in case the **space probe** comes into contact with a far-away planet where there is life!

Glossary

Astronauts People trained to travel or work in space.

Astronomer A person who studies space, often using telescopes.

Atmosphere The gases that surround a star, planet or moon.

Canyon A long, deep river valley.

Earth years A year is the time it takes for a planet to orbit the Sun. An Earth year is 365 days long.

Hubble Space Telescope A telescope that orbits the Earth. Its pictures of space are very clear because it is outside of Earth's atmosphere.

Hydrogen gas A very light gas. The Sun is also made of Hydrogen.

Liquid Something that flows easily.

Methane gas A colourless gas with no smell. It burns easily.

Orbit The path that a planet or other object takes around the Sun, or a satellite takes around a planet.

Solar system The Sun and everything that is in orbit around it.

Space probe A spacecraft sent from Earth to explore the solar system.

Year The time it takes for a planet to orbit the Sun once.

Index